TREVOR WYE

Beginner's Book
for the
Flute
PART ONE

TREVOR WYE

Beginner's Book for the Flute

PART ONE

Order No. NOV120584

Novello Publishing Limited
8/9 Frith Street, London W1V 5TZ

DISTRIBUTED BY

HAL•LEONARD®
CORPORATION
7777 W. BLUEMOUND RD. P.O. BOX 13819
MILWAUKEE, WISCONSIN 53213

Illustrations by Gordon Davies A.R.A.

Cover by Art and Design

Reprinted 1985, 1986, 1987, 1988, 1990, 1992, 1993, 1995, 1996, 1999, 2000, 2002

Now available from Novello:

PLAY THE FLUTE: a beginner's guide
A Novello Video (Colour: 35 minutes)
Presented by Trevor Wye
Order No: NOV 640001

This innovative video is intended to be a self-contained guide to the
fundamentals of flute playing, but students are sure to benefit from the use
of the video in conjunction with the publication on which it is based,
A Beginner's Book for the Flute (Part 1, Part 2 and Piano Accompaniments).

Also available from Novello:

A Practice Book for the Flute by Trevor Wye

This highly successful series of Practice Books for the Flute has proved to
be of tremendous value to players of all grades from beginners to advanced
students. Each book has a dependence upon the others and concentrates
on an individual facet of flute playing in detail. Collectively they form a
broad reference to the technical difficulties of the instrument, without con-
centrating on any one particular method of study.

The six volumes deal with:

Volume 1   TONE
Volume 2   TECHNIQUE
Volume 3   ARTICULATION
Volume 4   INTONATION AND VIBRATO
Volume 5   BREATHING AND SCALES
Volume 6   ADVANCED PRACTICE

For Kate Hill

PREFACE

Any new book appearing on the market usually boasts of new ideas and new format. This book is no different in this respect though it does incorporate all the well-tried recipes of the past.

Technically, the flute is the easiest of the woodwind instruments and one which lends itself most readily to being learnt chromatically. It is easier for a beginner to play in different keys, provided that the learning of each new note is given equal emphasis.

The general outline of this book is, therefore, to encourage:
  (a) enjoyment of flute playing and music making in the broadest sense.
  (b) familiarity with the lesser-known keys which, in turn, results in easier access to orchestras and ensembles.
  (c) the formation of a firm low register, the foundation to a good tone throughout the compass of the flute.
  (d) solo and ensemble playing.

The 72 numbered pieces (1-42 are in PART I, the rest in PART II) in this book can mostly be played either:
  1) as a solo
  2) as a duet
  3) as a solo with piano
  4) as a duet with piano
  5) as a solo or duet with guitar accompaniment.

The book of piano accompaniments, in which chord symbols are given, are up to Grade VI (Associated Board) in standard (though many are easier), and is available separately.

The book is intended for both individual and group tuition. It can be used without a teacher if circumstances make this necessary though a pupil is strongly advised to consult a good teacher.

Many exercises and tunes are by the author.

Piano accompaniments by Robert Scott with nine original pieces specially composed by Alan Ridout.

Finally, I acknowledge with grateful thanks, the players and teachers who have advised me on the preparation of this book:

Lucy Cartledge, Catharine Hill, Malcolm Pollack, Rosemary Rathbone, Alastair Roberts, Lenore Smith, Robin Soldan, Hilary Taggart, Stephanie Tromans, Lindsay Winfield-Chislett and Janet Way.

TREVOR WYE

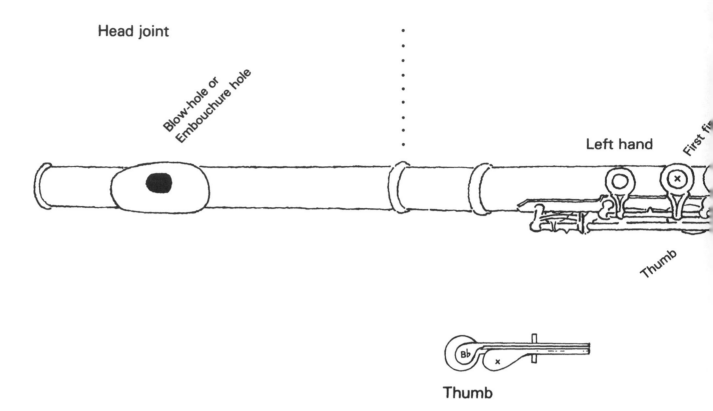

Head joint

Blow-hole or
Embouchure hole

Left hand

First fi

Thumb

Thumb

Blowing the headjoint

Take the headjoint and place the palm of the right hand across the open end of the tube to make it airtight. Place the lip plate against the lower lip so that less than half of the blow-hole is covered. The headjoint will be parallel with the lips. Bring the lips together and blow across the hole.

When a sound has been made, take the right hand away and try again. Be patient if you do not get an immediate result.

Try not to lose too much air.

Try to keep the sound steady. Repeat the above starting the note with the tongue as if making the syllable *te*. Do not end the note with your tongue. When successful: assemble the flute holding it as in the above diagram. See that the blow-hole is in line with the key for the first finger of the left hand. Note the footjoint position.

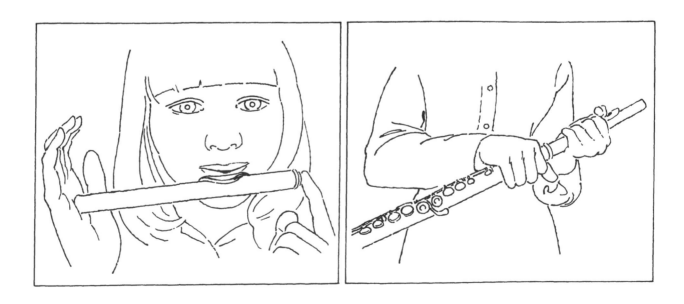

Body joint .... **Foot joint**

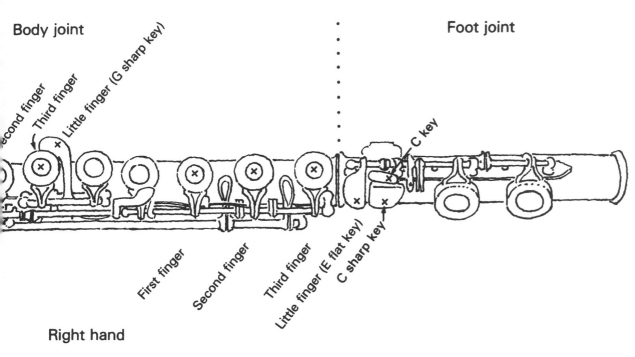

Second finger
Third finger
Little finger (G sharp key)

First finger
Second finger
Third finger
Little finger (E flat key)
C sharp key
C key

Right hand

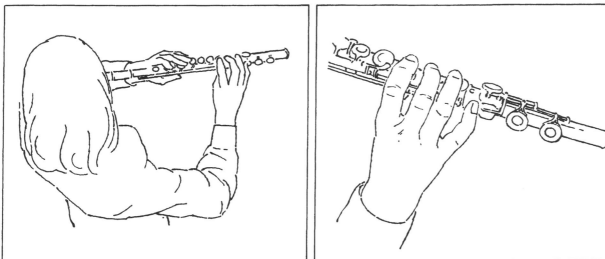

Study the pictures: notice the angle of the flute in relation to the body. Place the right and left hands on the flute as in the drawings above. Place your fingers on the flute as in the drawings above. Keep the little finger curved.

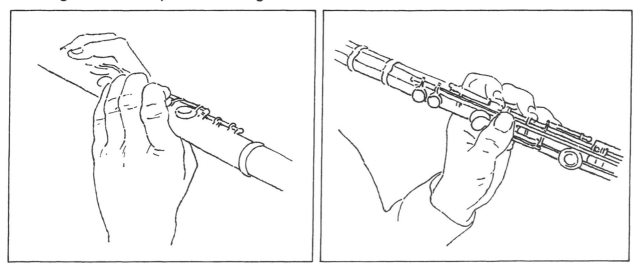

Left hand position
The left hand first finger curves under the flute to support it whilst the fingers curve over the keys. Notice the left hand thumb. Keep the thumb on the right lever.

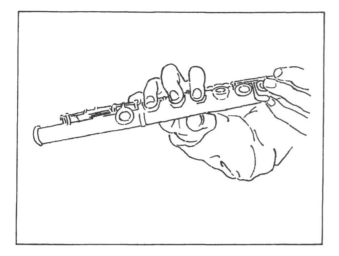

Right hand position

Hold up your right arm with the hand limp. Notice that the fingers are curved. Notice also that the thumb is sideways-on to the first finger. Place the hand over the flute without changing this relationship between the thumb and the hand. Place the curved fingers on the keys and the little finger on its key. The fingers should be at right angles to the flute: not pointing to the left or right.

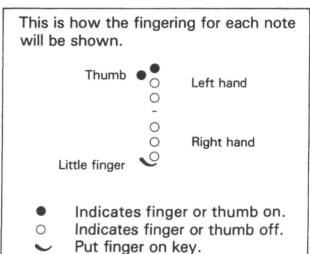

This is how the fingering for each note will be shown.

Thumb — Left hand

Right hand

Little finger

●   Indicates finger or thumb on.
○   Indicates finger or thumb off.
⌣   Put finger on key.

Blowing the flute

Always stand when playing. Holding the flute in front of you, turn your head about 45 degrees to the left and bring the flute to your head. Avoid bringing your head to the flute. Observe that your head and the flute are facing in a different direction to your shoulders.

Finger the note B

and play your first note.

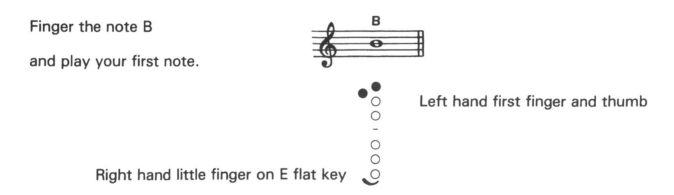

Left hand first finger and thumb

Right hand little finger on E flat key

Try to relax your arms and shoulders.

Breathing
Put the flute down and take a big breath *without raising the shoulders*. The stomach should expand followed by the chest. If you have any difficulty doing this, sit in an upright chair and hold on to the seat. Take another breath: this time the stomach should expand. Repeat without the aid of the chair.

Some don'ts:
1) Don't *end* the note with the tongue.
2) Don't push the flute hard against the mouth to stop it slipping down: tuck the left hand first finger a little under the flute. If the flute is slippery, glue some paper on the place where your first finger should go. Keep the left elbow down.
3) Keep the shoulders down when playing and when taking a breath.
4) Don't allow the flute to be supported on a *flat* right hand thumb: it causes the fingers to adopt a strained position and straightens the little finger. Keep the little finger bent (see picture below and on page 3).
5) Don't practice with your music on a table: if you haven't a music stand, support it using picture hooks and paper clips, or prop it up on the inside of your flute case if necessary.

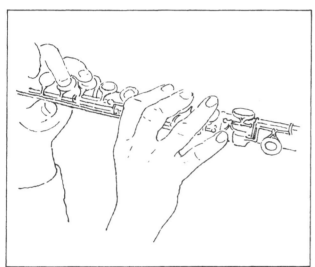

Incorrect right hand position

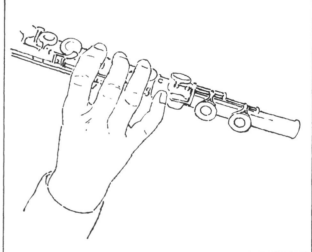

Correct right hand position

Practising
Practise every day. The lip muscles, tongue, fingers and breathing all need regular exercise if you are to progress quickly. If possible, try to practise at the *same time* each day. An athlete would soon pull a muscle if he trained only at weekends! Expression in music also needs regular practice.

Musical notes are named after the first seven letters of the alphabet.

They are placed on the *staff:*

This sign  is called a *treble clef* and shows that the instrument playing

from the staff is a high or *treble* instrument such as the descant and treble recorders, the violin and the flute.

Music is grouped into *bars* to show rhythmic stress or accent.

The *barline* shows the beginning and end of each bar.

barline

This final *double barline* (which may be thin or thick and thin) shows the end of a piece of music.

There are several different note lengths in music.

Here are some of them:

     𝅝   semibreve or whole-note

     𝅗𝅥   minim or half-note

     𝅘𝅥   crotchet or quarter-note

There are signs for silence which correspond to the note lengths. They are called rests.

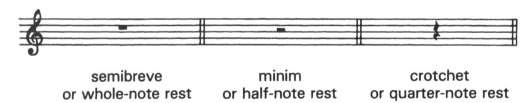

| semibreve | minim | crotchet |
| or whole-note rest | or half-note rest | or quarter-note rest |

Time-signatures
A time-signature, in the form of a fraction, is printed at the beginning of each piece to tell you what note values to expect in each bar throughout the piece.

Example:

$\frac{2}{4}$ = two quarter-notes or crotchets in each bar.

$\frac{3}{4}$ = three quarter-notes or crotchets in each bar.

$\frac{4}{4}$ = four quarter-notes (crotchets) or two half-notes (minims) in each bar.

Now take up your flute and play the exercise below counting four crotchet beats in each bar. Play the notes for their full length. You will use only one note: B.

Play the next exercise; each *minim* has two beats. Play the minims for their full length.

Play the next exercise; the time-signature shows three crotchet beats in each bar.

An exercise with a time-signature of $\frac{2}{4}$; two beats in a bar.

The following exercises contain notes of different values in each bar. Play the notes for their full length. Count carefully.

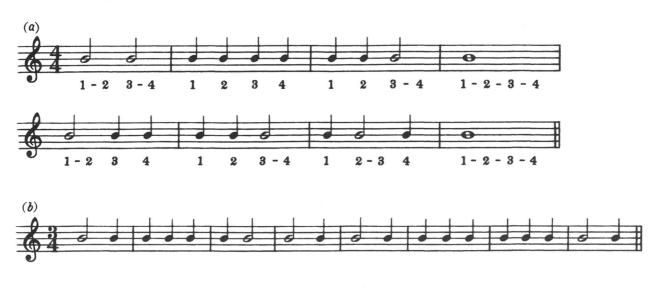

8

A Final exercise which uses both notes and rests:

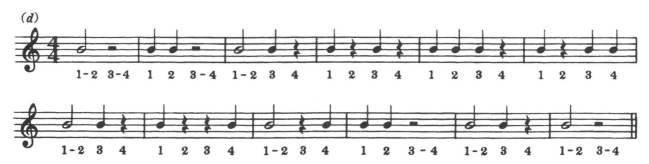

Play these exercises to develop a feeling for rhythm. They use only the one note you have learned: B. Do not end each note with the tongue.

If in doubt, sing the exercises, and count at the same time.

Introducing the first three notes B, A and G

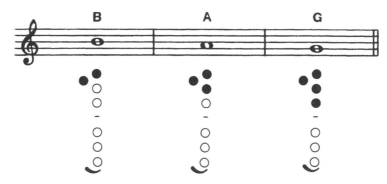

Tongue as if making the syllable *te* at the beginning of each note. It will give the note a clean start. Count carefully.

Remember to finger all the notes with the right hand little finger on the E flat key.

Do not use the *left* hand little finger yet.

WELSH MELODY

Like speech, music is divided into sentences and phrases. Try to make your breath last until the next breathing place. The music will then sound less broken up.

DUET

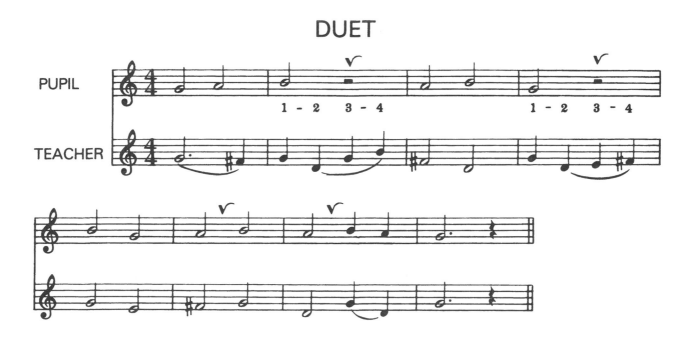

MERRILY WE ROLL ALONG

FINGER EXERCISE

Slurs

A *slur* is a curved line placed above or below a group of notes:

The notes are to be played in one breath tonguing only the *first* note. Count carefully when slurring.

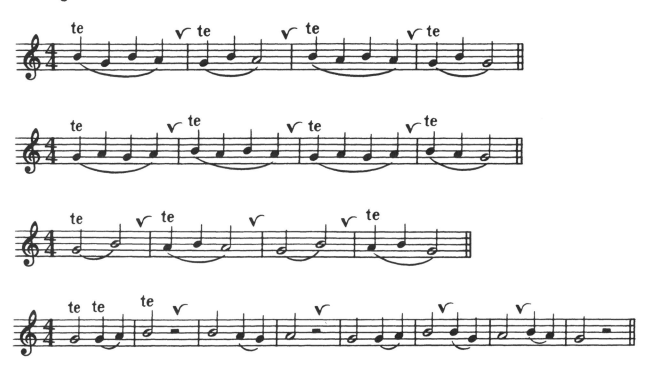

AU CLAIR DE LA LUNE

When two notes of the same name are connected with a curved line, their values are added together to make one continuous note. The line is called a *tie*. Don't tongue the second note.

So far, you have played in  4/4 time: four crotchet beats in a bar. This is sometimes called *common time* and is marked with a 𝄴 instead of 4/4 . Notice that the first beat of a bar always seems more important: it should, therefore, have a slight stress.

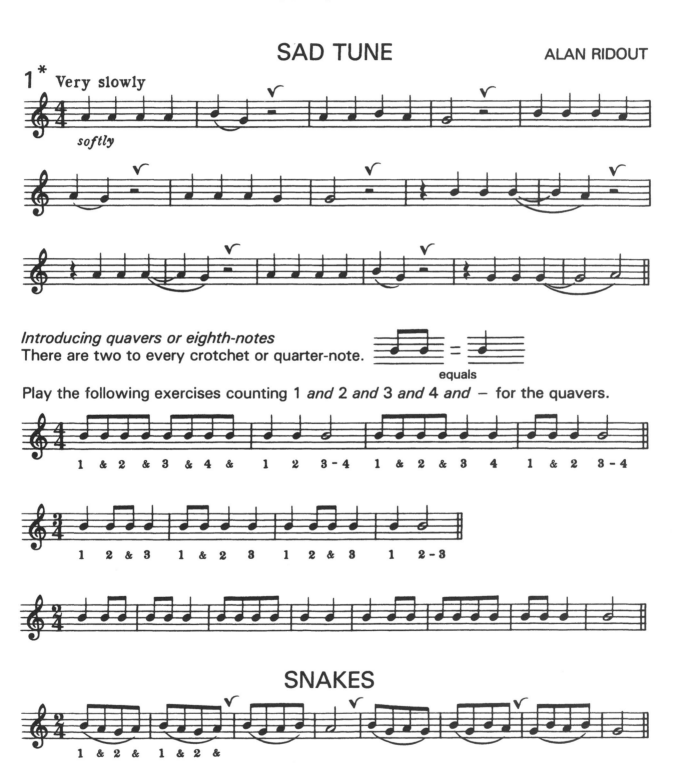

SAD TUNE

ALAN RIDOUT

1* Very slowly

softly

Introducing quavers or eighth-notes
There are two to every crotchet or quarter-note.

equals

Play the following exercises counting 1 *and* 2 *and* 3 *and* 4 *and* — for the quavers.

1 & 2 & 3 & 4 & 1 2 3 - 4 1 & 2 & 3 4 1 & 2 3 - 4

1 2 & 3 1 & 2 3 1 2 & 3 1 2 - 3

SNAKES

1 & 2 & 1 & 2 &

* All the *numbered* pieces have a piano accompaniment available separately.
The pieces sound better with piano or guitar accompaniment.

RAIN IS FALLING

1 & 2 & 1 - 2

This is a quaver rest:

Three tunes as a reading exercise

Whilst playing these tunes don't let the right hand fingers rest on the keywork.

(a)

1 & 2 1 & 2

(b) **Fairly quickly**

1 & 2 &

(c) **At a moderate speed**

Introducing C

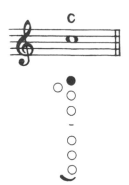

C

N.B. Don't be tempted to support the flute with the left thumb when C is played.

C

DUET

H. PURCELL

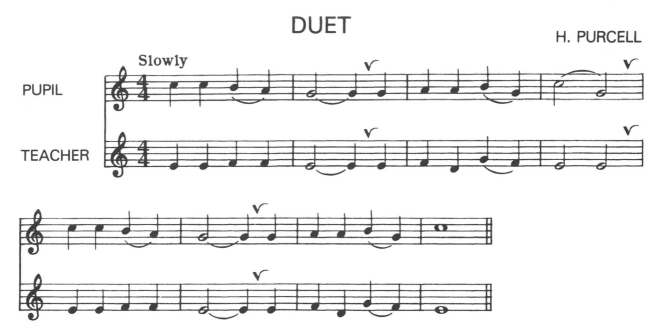

Most of the signs used to show speed in music are written at the start of each piece in Italian. From here onwards, the most common words will be given with the English translation repeated in brackets. For reference, there is a list at the back of the book.

2   AIR DE BUFFONS

16th century

$\frac{3}{4}$ time is three beats in a bar, as used in waltz time.

FINGER EXERCISE

Now check your posture and hand position with the pictures in the front of this book.

♩. This is a dotted minim: a dot after a note adds half its value to itself.

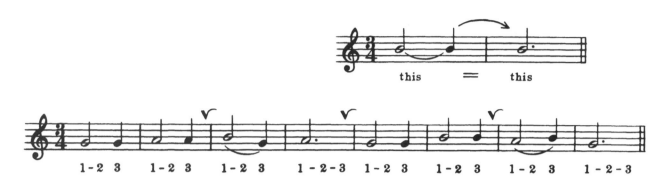

WALTZ

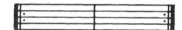

This is a repeat sign: repeat once all the music between these two signs. If there is only one set, repeat back to the beginning.

3   DANCE   SUSATO

1 The first flutes were made many thousands of years ago out of human bones, the tibia (leg bone) being a favourite. Until fairly recent times, tribes in South America would make flutes out of the bones, and drums out of the skins, of their defeated enemies, upon which to make music both to celebrate their victory and honour their foes.

Greek flute players were called Tibiscenes. One of them, Harmonides, in about 440 B.C., confessed to his teacher that his only motive in becoming a flute player was to gratify his vanity. His teacher said that the most certain way to acquire fame was to pay little heed to the many who know how to hiss, and to endeavour to gain the approval of the few who know how to judge. His words fell on deaf ears. At his first competition, Harmonides played with so many contortions and played so eagerly and blew so hard in order to gain popularity, that he suddenly fell dead.

All notes in music can be raised, or lowered, by placing a sign in front of them. The sign for raising a note is ♯ , a *sharp*. It raises the note against which it is placed. Its effect is cancelled by the barline.

Introducing G sharp
Fingering: as for G but add little finger of left hand.

FINGER EXERCISE

This is a pause sign: 𝄐 hold the note for a little longer than its written value.

pause 2nd time only

When a previously raised note needs to be restored back to its original sound, a natural sign (♮) is used.   Its effect is also cancelled by the barline. It is also sometimes used as a reminder.

G natural   reminder

4   MADRIGAL

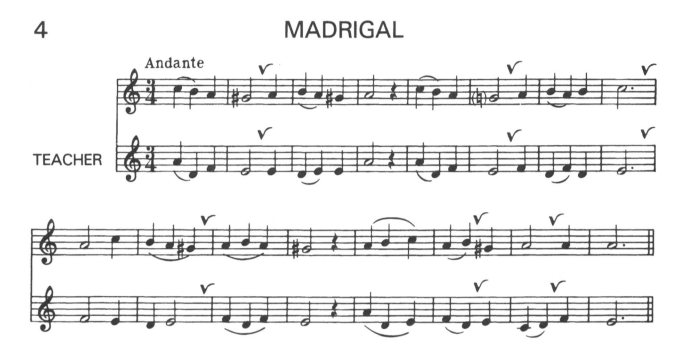

TEACHER

Work your fingers quickly and firmly on the keys even when playing slowly. Don't raise the fingers higher than necessary. This will help you develop good finger technique.

OLD LACE

Remember to finger all the notes with the right hand little finger on the E flat key.

HUNGARIAN FOLKSONG

18

Introducing F and E
Try not to let the tone get weaker as you play the low notes. Check your hand position with the pictures in the front of the book.

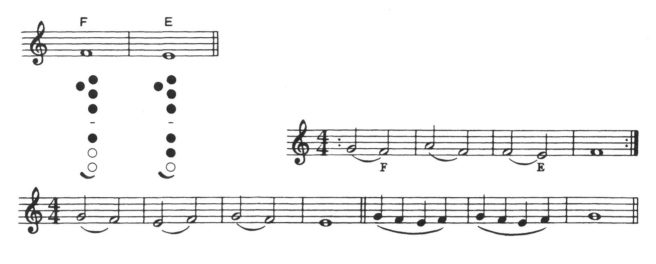

ALL THE NOTES

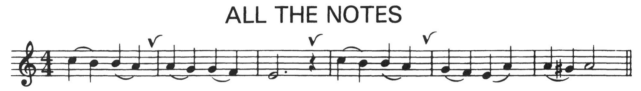

You have already played this familiar tune though using different notes:

AU CLAIR DE LA LUNE

Allegretto (fairly quickly)

LAVENDER

Moderato

WALKING

Moderato

Practise the same tune in **2/4** time. It should *sound* the same as in the previous time but with different stress.

WALKING

Moderato

A dot under or over a note means it should be played shorter than its written length or *staccato*. Don't *stop* the notes with the tongue.

STACCATO EXERCISE

Allegro

DANCE

Allegretto

A SHORT TUNE

Lento (slowly)

FINGER EXERCISE

MUFFINS

Vivace (lively)

Tone Development

The development of a beautiful tone is most important to your further progress. In these exercises — and in the exercises which follow — experiment with the speed of the air which you blow into your flute. Does increasing the air speed make a firmer tone? If it does, try: —

(a) decreasing the size of the hole in your lips through which you blow. Whilst obtaining a *clear* sound, try to be economical with the quantity of air used.

(b) moving the jaw backwards and forwards slightly, note any improvement. Play each note as long as possible. Take big breaths. Avoid turning the flute blow-hole in on your lip. *No more* than half should be covered. See the front of this book.

TONE EXERCISE

This piece starts with an incomplete bar. The note before the barline is called an *upbeat*. Notice how it affects the breathing places.

GERMAN DANCE

N.B. The last bar in German Dance is not complete. The remainder of that bar is contained in the upbeat at the start of the piece.

Introducing B flat
Remember that all notes can be both raised (♯), restored back to the original note (♮), and lowered: the sign to lower a note is called a flat (♭).

THE STOAT

MINUET

F major

In the last piece, there was a flat sign in front of every B. In the next piece, there is a B flat at the front of the piece to save writing a flat before every B. When sharps or flats appear at the *beginning* of a piece, it is called a *key-signature*.

Play the piece above *without* the B flats: it sounds rather odd. Notice how the piece seems to want to return to F at the end. This *key* – one flat – is called F Major. Later in the book you will be playing in other *keys.*

F major   ## MARCH   ANONYMOUS

Tone
Before starting the next pieces, play the first note of each piece as a long note to check the quality of your tone.

F major   ## NOW THE DAY IS OVER   S. BARING-GOULD

F major   ## JINGLE BELLS   J.S. PIERPOINT

In the next piece, notice that the phrases are three bars long; most phrases in music are four bars long. The phrases are indicated by brackets.

F major

5 THE NIGHTINGALE

FOLKSONG

F major

6 THE BEE

19th century

There are no sharps or flats in the key-signature of this next piece. It is in the key of C Major though it does change key during the piece which explains the G sharps. Pieces often change key or *modulate*. When a sharp, flat, or natural sign — which is not in the key-signature — appears in a piece, it is called an *accidental*. Its effect is cancelled by the barline.

C major

7 LULLABY

ALAN RIDOUT

SUR LE PONT D'AVIGNON

F major

FRENCH FOLKSONG

> This is an *accent*: the note over or under which it is placed is attacked strongly with the breath and tongue.

F major

8 THE CUCKOO

ANONYMOUS
?19th century

PUPIL I

PUPIL II

Practise your tone first before playing any of the pieces.

24

F major

FAREWELL

GERMAN
19th century

Scales are a series of notes which ascend and descend in ladder-like steps. They are important to the development of finger movements. Practise the exercises carefully and those that follow in the book.

FINGER EXERCISE

SCALE EXERCISE IN F MAJOR

F major

DANCE

PRAETORIUS

2 This native is whirling a bull-roarer, a primitive sort of flute. It makes a low humming noise. To make one you need: a piece of light wood 2½" x 18" (6.5 cm x 45 cm) ⅛" (½ cm) thick and about two yards of nylon string. Cut it to the shape in the drawing and round off the corners with sandpaper. Drill a hole ¾" (2 cm) from one end. Paint it, with decoration as shown, in bright emulsion. Tie a knot in the end of the string. Thread it through the hole. Whirl it around your head.

A tutor who tooted the flute
Tried to tutor two tooters to toot
Said the two to the tutor
Is it easier to toot
Or to tutor two tooters to toot?

Introducing F sharp

F sharp

The finger exercise has a new key-signature, G Major: it has one sharp, *F sharp*. All F's must be played as F sharp.

FINGER EXERCISE

G major

G major

Allegro

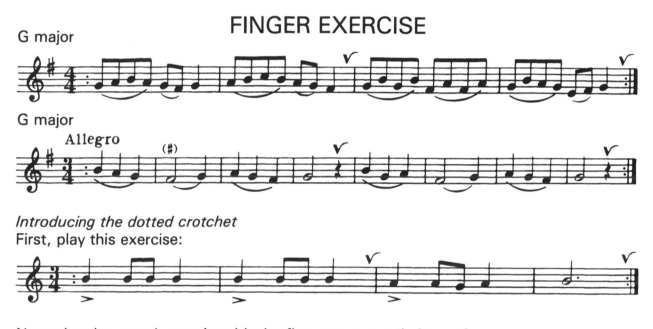

Introducing the dotted crotchet
First, play this exercise:

Now play the exercise again with the first *two* notes tied together:

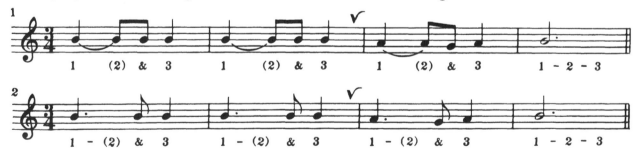

Exercises 1 and 2 should sound exactly the same. A dotted crotchet is equal to a crotchet *plus* a quaver.

NATIONAL ANTHEM

First and second time bars
Sometimes a repeated phrase has a different ending. Play the first six bars and repeat. On the second time through omit the *first-time* bar and play the *second-time* bar instead.

G major

11

MELODY

LULLY

Here is the same piece in another key: F major.

F major

12

MELODY

The signs and words to show the style and mood of a piece of music are traditionally written in Italian. Here are some of them:

forte (shortened to *f*): loudly
piano (shortened to *p*): softly
mezzo forte (shortened to *mf*): moderately loudly
mezzo piano (shortened to *mp*): moderately softly
crescendo (also written ——— or cresc.): gradually getting louder
diminuendo (also written ——— or dim.): gradually getting softer
rallentando (also shortened to rall.): gradually getting slower

Louder and softer:
You may have noticed that, when blowing softer, the note is lower in pitch. To prevent a note from becoming too flat, raise the air stream, when blowing softly, by pushing your jaw forward. Do the reverse when playing loudly. Always listen carefully and adjust the pitch if it doesn't sound right.

Count carefully

F major

13   RUSTIC DANCE

ALAN RIDOUT

Introducing E flat and D
N.B. For D — no little finger on E♭ key

Once again: check your right hand position.

Another name for E flat is D sharp though it is fingered in the same way. All the notes have more than one name. For a full explanation see page 54. PART II

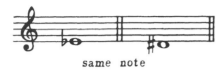

same note

LOW NOTE EXERCISE

A key-signature can indicate both a *major* and a *minor* key. Play the two tunes below and notice the different musical flavour.

Even though both tunes have the same key-signature, each one progresses to a different note at the end.

SCALE EXERCISE IN D MINOR

Here are two more. Minor-key tunes most often have an accidental.

SCALE EXERCISE IN E MINOR

THE MAIDEN

E minor
14

DANCE

E minor

SUSATO

Introducing C sharp

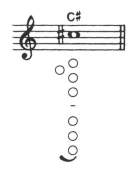

Be sure to support the flute correctly with the left hand.
See the pictures in the front of this book.

C sharp

The key of E major: F♯, C♯, G♯ and D♯.

SCALE EXERCISE IN E MAJOR

JINGLE BELLS

E major
J.S. PIERPOINT

32

E major

15

SAD WALTZ

18th century

SCALE EXERCISE IN D MAJOR

D major

16

THIS OLD MAN

The key here is A major with three sharps: F♯, C♯ and G♯.

SCALE EXERCISE IN A MAJOR

A major

FINGER EXERCISE

A major

A DANCE

17 Allegretto

An exercise and piece in the key of F♯ minor which has three sharps: F♯, C♯ and G♯.

SCALE EXERCISE IN F♯ MINOR

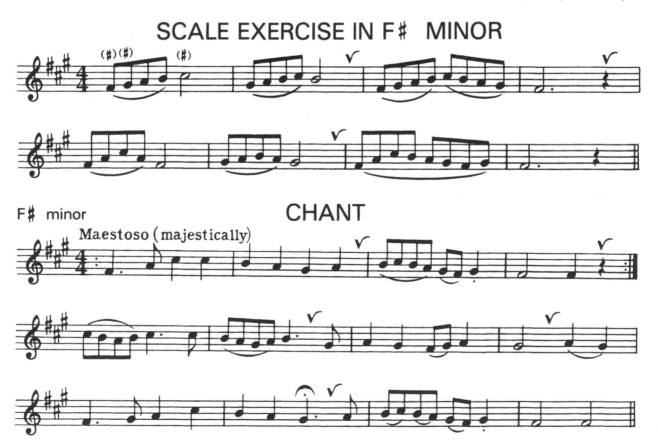

F♯ minor

CHANT

Maestoso (majestically)

34

You have already played this piece in another key.

E major
18 A DANCE
PRAETORIUS

F major
POLLY WOLLY DOODLE
AMERICAN

The new note in this piece is in fact an old note! *A sharp* is another name for B flat. For a full explanation see page 54 PART II.

Finger the A♯ as for B♭.   Count carefully.

E minor
19 AIR
ALAN RIDOUT

Introducing upper D

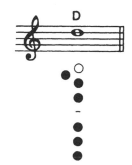

No little finger on key.

SCALE EXERCISE IN G MAJOR

G major

20   **BRANSLE**

GERVAISE

3 The classical Chinese flute, the Tse. Our modern flutes are descended from this simple bamboo flute which has been in use in China for several thousand years.

'No more the wily note is heard from his full flute, The riving air that tames the snake, Decoys the bird worries the she-wolf from her lair'

T. G. Hake (1809)

The oars were silver, which to the tune of flutes, kept stroke.

SHAKESPEARE (Anthony and Cleopatra)

A canon is a piece in which the second part exactly imitates the first part.

G major

21

NOEL: *A CANON*

CHEDEVILLE

This is a Round: player II starts when player I reaches the figure 2. Player III starts when player I reaches the figure 3, and so on. Keep repeating until tired of it!

LONDON'S BURNING

Round in four parts

This time-signature means two *minim* beats in a bar.

It is most often used in broad slow pieces or in march time.

F major

22

MELCHIOR FRANCK

Phrasing
Notice how the breathing marks divide the music into phrases just as in our speech. The signs described earlier (f and p, cresc. etc.) are now going to be used much more in the pieces which you will play. This will help the phrasing.

SCALE EXERCISE IN G MINOR

G minor

23   SWEDISH FOLK SONG

TONE EXERCISE

DA CAPO (shortened to *D.C.*) means go back to the beginning. You will often find the instruction *D.C. al FINE*.

G minor

DUDLEY'S GRUNT

24

Go back to the beginning and end at the *FINE* or finish bar.

G major

GERMAN DANCE

25

SCHUBERT

F major
26

FOLK TUNE

ALAN RIDOUT

Con moto (with motion)

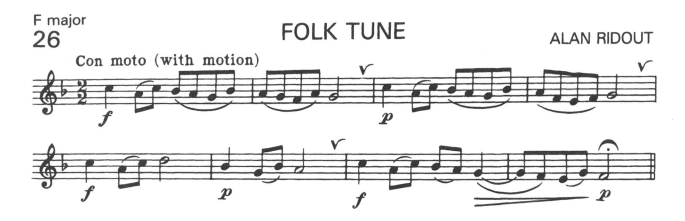

So far you have learned the notes from D to D' covering eight letter names: D E F G A B C and D'. This span of eight notes is called an octave. For the new notes – E and F – in the second octave, use a faster air speed or they will slip down to the lower octave. Raise the air stream slightly by moving the lower jaw forward. Use the same fingering as the lower octave.

Introducing upper E and F

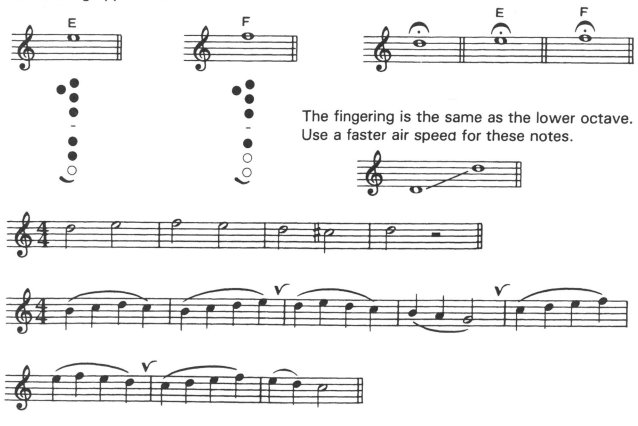

The fingering is the same as the lower octave. Use a faster air speed for these notes.

SCALE EXERCISE IN A MINOR

A minor

27 COVENTRY CAROL

Melody arranged by
MARTIN SHAW

Lento con moto (slowly with motion)

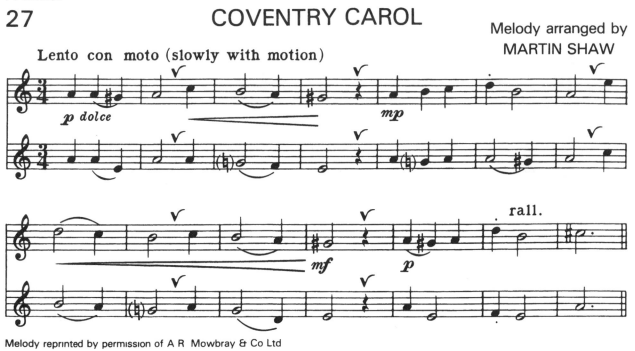

This time-signature also means two *minim* beats in a bar: ($\mathbb{C}$)

G major

28 ALLEMANDE

GERVAISE

SCALE EXERCISE IN A MAJOR

This short line above a note is a *tenuto* accent: it is a gentle accent and also means that the note is held for its full value.

A major

29

LORD HAYE'S MASQUE

CAMPION

Read again the notes on Tone Development on page 19.

TONE EXERCISE

E minor

30

OLD FRENCH CAROL

TRADITIONAL

Andante sostenuto (slowly and sustained)

p tranquillo (peacefully)

rall.

SCALE EXERCISE IN F MAJOR

G minor

31

RUSSIAN FOLK SONG

Vivace

FINE

mf

D.C. al Fine

rall.

F major
32 WITCHES' DANCE
18th century

4 The God Pan is playing pan-pipes, another ancient form of the flute. Its invention was thus: Pan fell in love with a beautiful maiden called Syrinx, though she ran away from him and hid in some reeds on a river bank. Pan slashed at the reeds and, not finding her, bound a bunch of canes together to make a flute on which to express his woe. Their love had been uneven, so the length of canes remained uneven: she who was once a beautiful maiden became a musical pipe!

G minor

33 RONDO

SUSATO

Introducing E flat or D sharp

E♭ is the same fingering as the low register, but with the first finger L.H. raised.

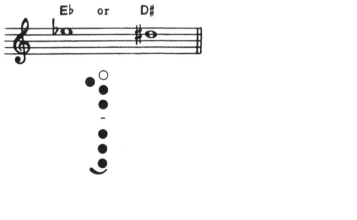

Check the tuning of your octaves.

SCALE EXERCISE IN Bᵇ MAJOR

Bᵇ major

34

O LITTLE ONE SWEET

17th century

Bb major

35 RONDO

SUSATO

Turn the book upside down!

FIRST PART

DUET

ANON.

SECOND PART

G minor

36 MARCH

MELCHIOR FRANCK

Introducing upper F sharp and G

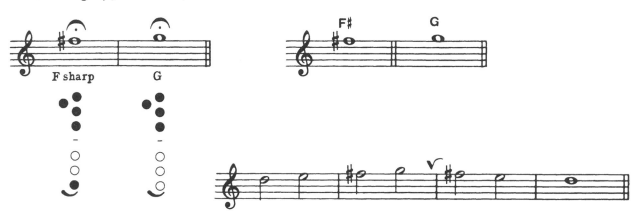

Check the tuning of your octaves.

SCALE EXERCISE IN G MAJOR

50

G major

37

MAYPOLE DANCE

TRADITIONAL

SCALE EXERCISE IN B MINOR

B minor

38

GREENSLEEVES

TRADITIONAL

SCALE EXERCISE IN C MAJOR

C major
39 Allegro RIGADOON
H. PURCELL

C major
40 Allegro DING DONG! MERRILY ON HIGH
16th century

A new key, F minor with four flats, B♭, E♭, A♭ – which is played with the same fingering as G sharp – and D♭ which is the same fingering as C sharp. See page 54 PART II for full explanation.

SCALE EXERCISE IN F MINOR

TAMBOURIN

F minor

41

RAMEAU

G minor

42

BRANLE

GERVAISE

$\frac{4}{2}$ time is four minim beats in a bar. This tune can be played by eight players. If only four players are used, leave out the even numbered entries.

CANON

TALLIS

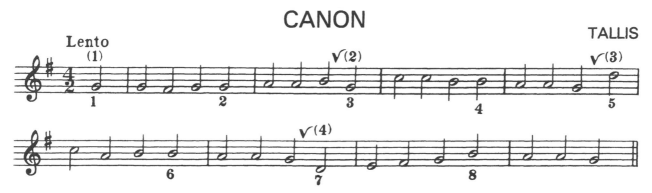

Check your right hand position described in the front of this book.

The soft complaining flute
In dying note discovers
The woes of helpless lovers.

DRYDEN

5 This piece of porcelain depicts a pipe-and-tabor player of the 17th century. These pipes — still obtainable today — can play many tunes on just three finger holes. The blowing end of the pipe has a mouthpiece like a recorder.

A list of Italian words and their meanings

Allegro	quickly
Allegretto	less quickly than Allegro
Andante	slowly
Andantino	less slow than Andante, though some composers use it to mean less *fast* (or slower), than Andante. Use your own judgment.
A tempo	in the original time (after slowing down)
Animato	animated
Al fine	to the finish (after D.C.)
Con spirito	with spirit
Crescendo (cresc.)	gradually getting louder
Con	with
Con moto	with motion
Diminuendo (dim.)	gradually getting softer
Dolce	sweetly
D.C. (da capo)	go back to the beginning
Fine	the finish
Forte (f)	loudly
Grazioso	gracefully
Larghetto	less slow than largo
Maestoso	majestically
Mezzo forte (mf)	half, or moderately loud
Mezzo piano (mp)	half, or moderately soft
Mesto	sadly
Moderato	at a moderate speed
Ritenuto (rit.)	holding back
Rallentando (rall.)	gradually getting slower
Sostenuto	sustained
Simile	continue in the same way
Tempo	time
Tempo di minuetto	in a minuet time
Tempo di Valse	in waltz time
Vivo	very quickly and lively
Vivace	lively

NOW YOU ARE READY FOR PART II

APPENDIX

Scale and arpeggio requirements for the Associated Board, Grades 1 and 2; to be played both tongued and slurred.

MUSIC FOR FLUTE

TUTORS

WYE, Trevor
A BEGINNER'S BOOK FOR THE FLUTE
A PRACTICE BOOK FOR THE FLUTE:
VOLUME 1 Tone (Cassette also available)
VOLUME 2 Technique
VOLUME 3 Articulation
VOLUME 4 Intonation and vibrato
VOLUME 5 Breathing and scales
VOLUME 6 Advanced Practice
PROPER FLUTE PLAYING

SOLO

ALBUM
ed Trevor Wye
MUSIC FOR SOLO FLUTE
This attractive collection draws together under
one cover 11 major works representing the
fundamental solo flute repertoire, edited in a
clear and practical form.

trans Gordon Saunders
EIGHT TRADITIONAL JAPANESE PIECES
Gordon Saunders has selected and transcribed
these pieces for tenor recorder solo or flute from
the traditional folk music of Japan.

FLUTE AND PIANO

ALBUMS
arr Barrie Carson Turner
CHRISTMAS FUN BOOK
CLASSICAL POPS FUN BOOK
ITALIAN OPERA FUN BOOK
MOZART FUN BOOK
POP CANTATA FUN BOOK
POPULAR CLASSICS FUN BOOK
RAGTIME FUN BOOK
TV THEME FUN BOOK

arr Trevor Wye
A VERY EASY BAROQUE ALBUM, Vols. 1 & 2
A VERY EASY CLASSICAL ALBUM
A VERY EASY ROMANTIC ALBUM
A VERY EASY 20TH CENTURY ALBUM
A FIRST LATIN-AMERICAN FLUTE ALBUM
A SECOND LATIN-AMERICAN FLUTE ALBUM

BENNETT, Richard Rodney
SUMMER MUSIC

COUPERIN, François
arr Trevor Wye
A COUPERIN ALBUM

ELGAR, Edward
arr Trevor Wye
AN ELGAR FLUTE ALBUM

FRASER, Shena
SONATINA

GALWAY, James
THE MAGIC FLUTE OF JAMES GALWAY
SHOWPIECES

HARRIS, Paul
CLOWNS

HURD, Michael
SONATINA

McCABE, John
PORTRAITS

RAMEAU, Jean Philippe
arr Trevor Wye
A RAMEAU ALBUM

REEMAN, John
SIX FOR ONE

SATIE, Erik
arr Trevor Wye
A SATIE FLUTE ALBUM

SCHUBERT, Franz
arr Trevor Wye
THEME AND VARIATIONS D.935 No.3

SCHURMANN, Gerard
SONATINA

VIVALDI, Antonio
arr Trevor Wye
A VIVALDI ALBUM

Printed in Great Britain by Printwise (Haverhill) Limited, Suffolk 08/02 (44994)